www.capstonepub.com
Visit our website to find out
more information about
Heinemann-Raintree books.

To order:
☎ Phone 800-747-4992
💻 Visit www.capstonepub.com
to browse our catalog and order online.

© 2013 Heinemann Library
an imprint of Capstone Global Library, LLC
Chicago, Illinois

Edited by Daniel Nunn, Rebecca Rissman, and Sian Smith
Designed by Cynthia Della-Rovere
Picture research by Mica Brancic
Production by Victoria Fitzgerald
Originated by Capstone Global Library Ltd
Printed and bound in China by South China Printing
Company Ltd

16 15 14 13 12
10 9 8 7 6 5 4 3 2 1

Library of Congress Cataloging-in-Publication Data
Nunn, Daniel.
   Numbers in Spanish : Los Números / Daniel Nunn.
      p. cm.—(World languages-Numbers.)
   Includes bibliographical references and index.
   ISBN 978-1-4329-6673-7 (hb)—ISBN 978-1-4329-6680-5 (pb) 1.
Spanish language—Textbooks for foreign speakers—English—Juvenile
literature. 2. Counting—Juvenile literature. I. Title.
   PC4129.E5N88 2012
   468.2'421—dc23
                              2011050547

Acknowledgments
We would like to thank Shutterstock for permission to reproduce
photographs: © Agorohov, © Aleksandrs Poliscuks, © Alex James Bramwell,
© Andreas Gradin, © Andrey Armyagov, © archidea, © Arogant, © atoss,
© Baloncici, © Benjamin Mercer, © blackpixel, © charles taylor, © Chris
Bradshaw, © cloki, © dcwcreations, © DenisNata, © Diana Taliun, © Eric
Isselée, © Erik Lam, © Fatseyeva, © Feng Yu, © g215, © Hywit Dimyadi, ©
Iv Nikolny, © J. Waldron, © jgl247, © joingate, © karam Miri, © Karkas, ©
kedrov, © LittleMiss, © Ljupco Smokovski, © Lori Sparkia, © Max Krasnov,
© Michelangelus, © Mike Flippo, © mimo, © Nordling, © Olga Popova,
© Pavel Sazonov, © pics fine, © Rosery, © Ruth Black, © Shmel, © Stacy
Barnett, © Steve Collender, © Suzanna, © Tania Zbrodko, © topseller, ©
Vasina Natalia, © Veniamin Kraskov, © Vinicius Tupinamba, © Volodymyr
Krasyuk, © Vorm in Beeld, © Winston Link, © xpixel.

Cover photographs reproduced with permission of Shutterstock: number 1
(© Leigh Prather), number 2 (© Glovatskiy), number 3 (© Phuriphat).
Back cover photograph of three chairs reproduced with permission of
Shutterstock (© Alex James Bramwell).

We would like to thank Rebeca Otazua Bideganeta and Silvia Vázquez-
Fernández for their invaluable assistance in the preparation of this book.

Contents

Uno 2

Dos 4

Tres 6

Cuatro 8

Cinco 10

Seis 12

Siete 14

Ocho 16

Nueve 18

Diez 20

Dictionary 22

Index and Notes 24

Uno

un perro

Hay un perro.

un suéter

Hay un suéter.

Dos

un gato

Hay dos gatos.

Hay dos zapatos.

Tres

una chica

Hay tres chicas.

una silla

Hay tres sillas.

Cuatro

un pájaro

Hay cuatro pájaros.

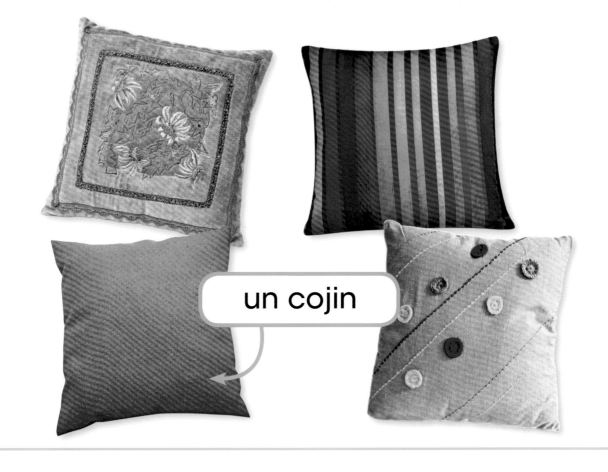

un cojin

Hay cuatro cojines.

Cinco

un juguete

Hay cinco juguetes.

un libro

Hay cinco libros.

Seis

un abrigo

Hay seis abrigos.

un lápiz

Hay seis lápices.

Siete

una naranja

Hay siete naranjas.

una galleta

Hay siete galletas.

Ocho

un coche

Hay ocho coches.

un sombrero

Hay ocho sombreros.

Nueve

un globo

Hay nueve globos.

una vela

Hay nueve velas.

Diez

una manzana

Hay diez manzanas.

una flor

Hay diez flores.

Dictionary

See words in the "How To Say It" columns for a rough guide to pronunciations.

Spanish Word	How To Say It	English Word
abrigo / abrigos	abb-ree-go /abb-ree-gos	coat / coats
chica / chicas	chee-ca / chee-cas	girl / girls
cinco	thin-co	five
coche / coches	cotch-ay / cotch-ays	car / cars
cojin / cojines	co-jin /co-jin-es	cushion / cushions
cuatro	quat-tro	four
diez	dee-eth	ten
dos	doss	two
flor / flores	floor / floo-rays	flower / flowers
galleta / galletas	guy-etta/ guy-ettas	cookie / cookies
gato / gatos	ga-to /gat-os	cat / cats
globo / globos	glo-bo / glo-bos	balloon / balloons
hay	I (as in "pie")	there is / there are
juguete / juguetes	who-get-ay / who-get-ays	toy / toys
lápiz / lápices	laa-peeth / laa-pee-thays	pencil / pencils
libro / libros	lee-bro / lee-bros	book / books

Spanish Word	How To Say It	English Word
manzana / manzanas	man-than-na / man-than-nas	apple / apples
naranja / naranjas	na-ran-ha / na-ran-has	orange / oranges
nueve	noo-e-bay	nine
ocho	otch-o	eight
pájaro / pájaros	paa-ha-ro / paa-ha-ros	bird / birds
perro	per-ro	dog
seis	say-ees	six
siete	see-et-tay	seven
silla / sillas	see-ya / see-yas	chair / chairs
sombrero / sombreros	som`-brer-ro / som-brer-ros	hat / hats
suéter	sweater	sweater
tres	trayss	three
un / una	oo-n / oo-nah	a
un / una / uno	oo-n / oo-nah / oo-noh	one
vela / velas	bella / bellas	candle / candles
zapato / zapatos	tha-pat-o / tha-pat-os	shoe / shoes

Index

eight 16, 17

five 10, 11

four 8, 9

nine 18, 19

one 2, 3

seven 14, 15

six 12, 13

ten 20, 21

three 6, 7

two 4, 5

Notes for Parents and Teachers
In Spanish, nouns are either masculine or feminine. The word for "a" or "one" changes accordingly—either un (masculine) or una (feminine). "Uno" is used when you write the number one on its own rather than as part of a sentence.